1.1

Welcome to Reading!

Hello, Reader!

This year, you'll read many wonderful stories. You'll meet a pig in a wig and a bear on a bus!

As you read, you will achieve the **California standards.**

What are standards?

Turn the page and find out.

Meet the Standards Along the Way

Standards are goals. For example, one goal is to listen carefully. Another goal is to learn new words.

These goals can help you read and write well. Your teacher will help you. Your reading books will help you, too.

Many **standards** are listed before stories, like this.

Look for **standards** in other places in your books.

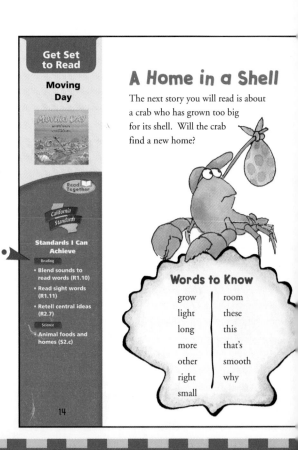

Get Set to Read

Moving Day

Read Together

California Standards

Standards I Can Achieve

Reading
- Blend sounds to read words (R1.10)
- Read sight words (R1.11)
- Retell central ideas (R2.7)

Science
- Animal foods and homes (S2.c)

14

A Home in a Shell

The next story you will read is about a crab who has grown too big for its shell. Will the crab find a new home?

Words to Know

grow	room
light	these
long	this
more	that's
other	smooth
right	why
small	

You Can Do It!

Each day, your reading and writing will get stronger. Before you know it, you'll reach the standards for first grade!

Practice Sentences

1. There is no more room to grow in this shell.
2. That's why I must find a new shell.
3. This one is too long.
4. This one is too light.
5. This one is too smooth.
6. These other small shells are not right!
7. This shell is the best match.

15

What else will you learn this year?
Let's find out!

Visit Worlds of Wonder!

Do you love animals? As you read, you'll see where animals live and how they grow.

You'll read about ducks, butterflies, and even tree frogs!

Sometimes you will use what you know about numbers.

You'll learn about people who live and work and play together.

Math

Science

History

You're On Your Way!
Do your best work.
Listen to those who
can help you learn.
The reading skills
you learn now will
travel with you all
your life.

HOUGHTON MIFFLIN

Reading

★ California ★

Here We Go!

Senior Authors
J. David Cooper
John J. Pikulski

Authors
Patricia A. Ackerman
Kathryn H. Au
David J. Chard
Gilbert G. Garcia
Claude N. Goldenberg
Marjorie Y. Lipson
Susan E. Page
Shane Templeton
Sheila W. Valencia
MaryEllen Vogt

Consultants
Linda H. Butler
Linnea C. Ehri
Carla B. Ford

HOUGHTON MIFFLIN
Reading
A Legacy of Literacy

HOUGHTON MIFFLIN   BOSTON · MORRIS PLAINS, NJ

California · Colorado · Georgia · Illinois · New Jersey · Texas

Cover and title page photography by Tony Scarpetta.

Cover illustration by Nadine Bernard Westcott.

Acknowledgments begin on page 263.

Printed in the U.S.A.

ISBN: 0-618-15158-3

789-DW-06 05 04

Contents
Theme 1

All Together Now 12

Big Book: Charles Tiger
by Siobhan Dodds

fantasy

realistic fiction

🎗 Award-winning author

fiction

🎗 Award-winning author and illustrator

Phonics Library:
Can It Fit?
Who Can Hit?
One Big Fat Fig

On My Way Practice Readers

Cat
by Alice Lisson

Fan Cat Can Jump
by Iris Littleman

One Big Hit
by Kathryn Lewis

Theme Paperbacks

Bear Play
by Miela Ford

Dan and Dan
by Marcia Leonard
photographs by
Dorothy Handelman

I Had a Hippopotamus
by Hector Viveros Lee

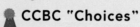
CCBC "Choices"

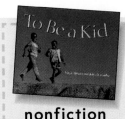

Surprise! 128

fantasy

Big Book: Minerva Louise at School
by Janet Morgan Stoeke
IRA/CBC Children's Choice
Bank Street College Best Children's
Books of the Year

realistic fiction

fantasy

Phonics Library:
Not Yet!
Big Ben
Get Wet, Ken!

Not Yet!
by Sid Jones
illustrated by Kelly Murphy

Len Hen can get one
kit in the tan van.

Big Book: Jasper's Beanstalk
*by Nick Butterworth and
Mick Inkpen*

fantasy

Best Books for Children
United Kingdom Children's Book Award

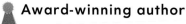

Phonics Library:
The Bug Kit
Quit It, Zig!
Rug Tug

The Bug Kit
by Lisa Crane
illustrated by Pamela R. Levy

Jen got a big bug kit.

On My Way
Practice Readers

Five Big Boxes
by Irma Singer

The Pet
by Maria Cara

Where Is Tug Bug?
by Oscar Gake

Theme Paperbacks

"What Is That?"
Said the Cat
by Grace Maccarone
illustrated by Jeffrey Scherer

The Pet Vet
by Marcia Leonard
photographs by
Dorothy Handelman

Spots
by Marcia Leonard
photographs by
Dorothy Handelman

To read about more good books, go to Education Place.

www.eduplace.com/kids

. . . .

This Internet reading incentive program provides thousands of titles for children to read.

www.bookadventure.org

All Together Now

Teacher Read Aloud

Because we do
All things together
All things improve,
Even weather.

**from the poem
"Together"
by Paul Engle**

The Cat Sat

Teacher Read Aloud

Standards I Can Achieve

Reading

- Blend sounds to read words (R1.10)
- Read sight words (R1.11)
- Identify sequence (R2.1)

Words to Know

go   cat
on   Sam
the   sat

Sam Cat sat.

14

Go, Sam Cat!

Sam Cat sat on the  girl .

15

Meet the Author and Illustrator
Lynn Munsinger

The Cat Sat

written and illustrated
by Lynn Munsinger

Sam Cat sat.

Go, Sam Cat!

Sam Cat sat.

Go, Sam Cat!

Sam Cat sat.

Go, Sam Cat!

Sam Cat sat on the .

girl

25

Think About the Story

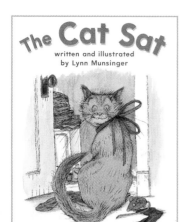

The Cat Sat
written and illustrated
by Lynn Munsinger

1 Why did the girl say, "Go, Sam Cat"?

2 What was the best place for the cat to sit?

3 How would you get the cat to move?

Write a Label

Draw and label a picture of the cat. Share your picture.

27

The Mat

The Mat

by Nadine Bernard Westcott

Teacher Read Aloud

California Standards

Standards I Can Achieve

Reading

- Blend sounds to read words (R1.10)
- Read sight words (R1.11)
- Identify sequence (R2.1)

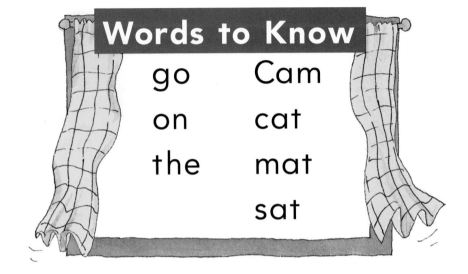

Words to Know

go   Cam

on   cat

the   mat

          sat

Cam Cat sat.

Cam Cat sat on the mat.

Go, Cam Cat!

Meet the
Author and Illustrator
Nadine Bernard Westcott

The Mat

by Nadine Bernard Westcott

Cam Cat sat on the mat.

33

Cat, Cat, Cat! Go, Cam Cat!

Cow sat.

35

36

 **sat.**

Goat

37

 **sat.**

Dog

38

Cam Cat sat.

Go!

Cam Cat!

The mat sat on Cam Cat.

Think About the Story

1 Why do you think the animals sat on the mat?

2 Why did the woman yell, "Go"?

3 Would you want animals in your house? Why?

Go, Cat!

Writing ▶

Write a Sign

Make a sign to help keep
the animals out of the house.

45

Cats

Cats are furry, cats are small
Cats are hardly big at all
Cats can purr and cats can mew
Do you like cats?
I sure do!

by Jacquiline Kirk, Age 9
Mauritius, Indian Ocean

At Night

When night is dark
my cat is wise
to light the lanterns
in his eyes.

by Aileen Fisher

illustrated by Lisa Campbell Ernst

California Standards

Standards I Can Achieve

Words to Know

and	Fan
here	fat
jump	Nan
not	pat
can	tap

Nan can jump.
Tap, tap, tap.
Fan can not jump.

Nan and Fan can go.

Nan can pat the fat, fat cat.
Pat, pat, pat.

Meet the Illustrator
Lisa Campbell Ernst

illustrated by Lisa Campbell Ernst

Nan can go.

Fan can not.

Nan can jump.
Tap, tap, tap.

Fan can not.

Nan can pat the fat, fat cat.
Pat, pat, pat.

Fan can not.

Nan can go.

Fan can not.

Fan, Fan, Fan!

Go, Fan!

Nan can go.

Fan can go.

Think About the Story

illustrated by Lisa Campbell Ernst

1 Why did Fan follow Nan?

2 Why can't Fan go to Nan's school?

3 What would you do if a pet followed you to school?

Write a List

Make a class list of pets. Write "Our Pets" at the top of the list.

65

written by Diane Hoyt-Goldsmith
photographs by Joel Benjamin

Words to Know

and	fan
here	Nat
too	Pam
we	Pat
can	

Pam can fan.

Pam and Pat can fan.

Nat can fan here, too.
We can fan!

Meet the Author
Diane Hoyt-Goldsmith

Meet the Photographer
Joel Benjamin

We Can!

written by Diane Hoyt-Goldsmith
photographs by Joel Benjamin

Can Nat, Pat, and Pam go?

Nat can. Pat can. Pam can.

Pam can go here.

Pat can, too.

Pam can read.

Pat can, too.

Pam can write.

Nat can, too.

Pam can draw.

Pat can, too.

Nat can, too.

Pam can fan! Nat can fan!
Pat can fan! We can fan!

Teacher
Read Aloud

Think About the Story

written by Diane Hoyt-Goldsmith
photographs by Joel Benjamin

1 What can the children do at school?

2 Do you think the children like school? Why?

3 Would you like to go to their school? Why?

82

Describe a Character

Use punch-out letters to make a character's name. Then write one word to describe the character.

The More We Get Together

The more we get together,
   together, together,
The more we get together,
   the happier we'll be.
'Cause your friends are my friends,
   and my friends are your friends,
The more we get together,
   the happier we'll be.

Traditional

The Big Hit

The **Big Hit**

written by
Angela Shelf
Medearis

illustrated by
John Ceballos

Teacher
Read Aloud

California
Standards

**Standards I Can
Achieve**

Reading

• **Blend sounds to
read words (R1.10)**

• **Read sight words
(R1.11)**

• **Make predictions
(R2.5)**

Words to Know

a	big
find	hit
have	ran
one	tag
who	Tim
bat	Tip

Who can find a
big, big bat?
Can Sam?

We have one big bat.

Pat can hit.
Can Tip hit?

Can Tim tag Sam?

Meet the Author
Angela Shelf Medearis

Meet the Illustrator
John Ceballos

89

The Big Hit

written by
Angela Shelf Medearis

illustrated by
John Ceballos

Who can find a big bat?

We have a big bat.

Who can hit?

93

Sam can hit.

Go, Sam! Sam ran.

Tim can not tag Sam.

Pat can hit.

Go, Pat! Pat ran.

99

Cam can not tag Pat.

Bam! Nat hit one big hit.

We ran, ran, ran!

Tip ran, ran, ran!

103

Think About the Story

The **Big Hit**

written by
Angela Shelf Medearis

illustrated by
John Ceballos

1 Do you think the children like to play ball? Why?

2 Why did the children chase Tip?

3 How would you get the ball from Tip?

104

Write a Name

Draw your favorite character from the story. Write the character's name.

by David McPhail

California
Standards

Standards I Can Achieve

Reading

- Blend sounds to read words (R1.10)

- Read sight words (R1.11)

- Retell central ideas (R2.7)

Words to Know

a	fig
find	fit
have	hat
one	pig
to	ran
who	sit
big	Tim

Who can find Big Pig?
Nan can. Can Tim?

Big Pig ran to Nan.

Sit, Big Pig.
Have one big, fat fig.

Can a hat fit Big Pig?

Meet the Author and Illustrator
David McPhail

Big Pig

by David McPhail

Chapter 1

Tim can go to a farm.
Nan can, too.

Tim and Nan find a big hat.

Can the big hat fit Tim?

Can the big hat fit Nan?

Who can the big hat fit?

The big hat can fit Big Pig.

Chapter 2

1. Feed Big Pig.
2. Sit on Big Pig.

Can Nan and Tim sit on Big Pig?

Big Pig can have one fat fig.

Nan can sit.

Big Pig can have a big carrot.

Tim can sit.

Go, Big Pig!

Big Pig ran!
Tim and Nan sat!

Think About the Story

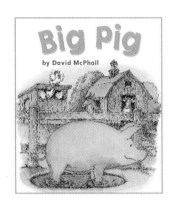

1 Why does Big Pig get the hat?

2 Why did Nan and Tim sit on Big Pig?

3 Would you like to visit Big Pig's farm? Why?

Writing

Write a Menu

What does Big Pig like to eat?
Draw a picture and label it.

There Was a Small

There was a small pig who wept tears
When his mother said,
   "I'll wash your ears."
As she poured on the soap,
He cried, "Oh, how I hope
This won't happen again for ten years!"

by Arnold Lobel

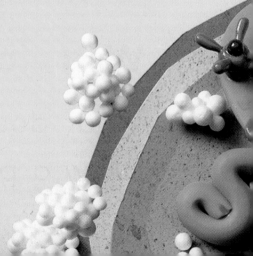

Pig Who Wept Tears

Surprise!

No matter where
  I travel,
No matter where
  I roam,
No matter where
  I find myself,
I always am
  at home.

**from the poem "Riddle"
by Mary Ann Hoberman**

129

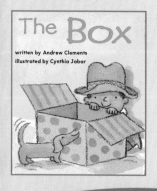

The Box

written by Andrew Clements
illustrated by Cynthia Jabar

Teacher Read Aloud

California Standards

Standards I Can Achieve

Reading

- **Blend sounds to read words (R1.10)**

- **Read sight words (R1.11)**

- **Respond to questions (R2.2)**

Words to Know

once	got
what	lot
box	on
Don	top
Dot	wig
fox	

Once Don and Dot got a big box. What can fit in the big box?

A wig can fit.
A fox can fit.
Can Don and Dot sit on top?

A lot can fit in the big box.

Meet the Author
Andrew Clements

Meet the Illustrator
Cynthia Jabar

The Box

written by Andrew Clements

illustrated by Cynthia Jabar

Once Don got a big box.

What can fit in the box?

One tan fox can fit.

One pig in a wig can fit.

One big hat can fit.

A lot can fit in the box.

Dot got the box.

What can Dot find in the box?

Dot can find a tan fox on top.

Dot can find a pig in a wig.

Dot can find a big hat.

Don and Dot can fit!
A lot can fit in a box!

Think About the Story

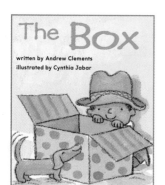

1 How many things did Don put in the box?

2 What might Dot do with the things in the box?

3 What would you put in the box?

146

Write a Description

Draw something you would put in the box. Write about your picture.

Words to Know

five	Don
four	Dot
three	Fox
two	got
upon	lot
what	Ox
box	wig
Dog	win

A big box sat upon a mat.
Can Dog win the big box?

 Dog got the box!
Fox got wig one.

 Ox got wig two.

 Cat got wig three.

 Dot got wig four.

 Don got wig five.

 What a lot in a big box!

Meet the Author and Illustrator
Valeria Petrone

Wigs in a Box

by Valeria Petrone

A big box sat upon a shelf.
Can Pat Pig win the box?

153

Pat Pig can win.
Pat Pig can hit the ball in.

Pat Pig got the big box!
What can Pat Pig find in it?

Pat Pig can find a wig.

Pat Pig can find five wigs
in the big box!

Wig one can fit Pat Pig.

Wig two can fit Dot Fox.

Wig three can fit Don Dog.

Wig four can fit Fat Cat.

Wig five can fit Tan Ox.

Thanks a lot, Pat Pig!

Think About the Story

1. What plan did Pat Pig make when he saw the wigs in the box?

2. Why did the animals thank Pat Pig?

3. Which wig would you choose?

Write a Character Description

Use punch-out letters to write your favorite character's name. Then write some words to tell about the character.

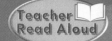
Here Is

Here is the beehive.
Where are the bees?

Hidden away where
nobody sees.

Watch and you'll
see them come
out of the hive.

166

the Beehive

One, two, three, four, five.

Bzzzzzzzz . . .
all fly away!

What Can a Vet Do?

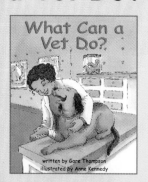

What Can a Vet Do?

written by Gare Thompson
illustrated by Anne Kennedy

Teacher
Read Aloud

California
Standards

Standards I Can Achieve

Reading

- Blend sounds to read words (R1.10)

- Read sight words (R1.11)

- Use context for understanding (R2.4)

Words to Know

do	Ned
for	pen
is	pet
my	van
Ben	vet
get	wet
kit	yes

Ben is my pet.
Ben can not get wet.

Is Ben at the vet?
Ben is not at the vet yet.

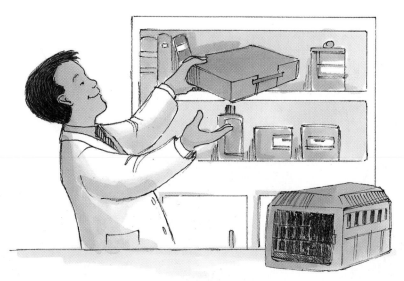

Ben can get in a pen.
A vet can get a kit.
What can a vet do for Ben?

Gare Thompson

Meet the Illustrator
Anne Kennedy

What Can a Vet Do?

written by Gare Thompson
illustrated by Anne Kennedy

171

Chapter 1

What bit my pet cat Big Ben?

Get Big Ben to the vet!

Can the vet fix Big Ben?
The vet can get a kit.

Big Ben can sit.

Big Ben can get wet.

The vet can pat Big Ben.

Yes, the vet can do a lot
for Big Ben!

Chapter 2

Ned is my big pet.
Ned is in a big pen.

Mom, get the vet!

Ned can not jump.

Here is the vet in a tan van.

The vet can get a big kit.
Can the vet fix Ned?

Yes, the vet can fix Ned!

A vet can do a lot.

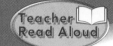
Think About the Story

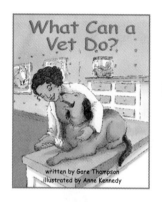

What Can a
Vet Do?

written by Gare Thompson
illustrated by Anne Kennedy

1 What does a vet do?

2 How do you know the girl and the boy care about their pets?

3 Would you like to be a vet? Why?

Write a Description

Draw a picture of a pet at the vet.
Write about your picture.

Hot Fox Soup

HOT FOX SOUP

by
SATOSHI KITAMURA

Teacher
Read Aloud

California Standards

Standards I Can Achieve

Reading

- Blend sounds to read words (R1.10)
- Read sight words (R1.11)
- Use context for understanding (R2.4)

Words to Know

I	Hen
is	kit
me	let
my	met
said	vat
you	wet
get	yes
	yet

Hen got a big kit.
Hen got a big vat.
Hen met Fox.

"What can I get?" said Fox.
"You can get wet," said Hen.
"Here is my vat. Get in."
"Not me!" said Fox.

"Yes," said Hen. "Get wet!"
"Not yet!" said Fox.

Meet the Author
and Illustrator

Satoshi Kitamura

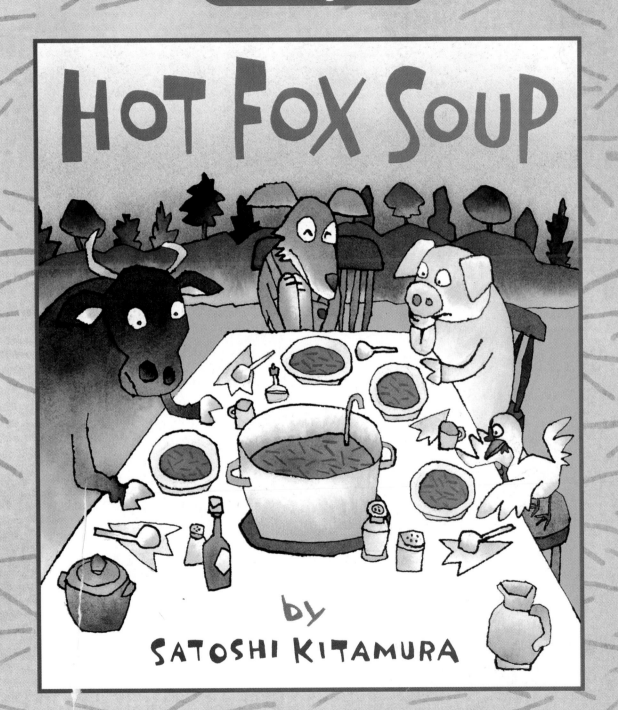

HOT FOX SOUP

by

SATOSHI KITAMURA

Fox wanted hot hen soup.

Fox got a big, big vat.
Fox lit a hot, hot fire.

Fox got a noodle soup kit in a box.

Fox met Hen.
"What can I get?" said Hen.

"Get wet in my vat, Hen," said Fox.

"Not me!"
Hen ran.

Fox met Pig.

Fox wanted hot pig soup.

"What can I get?" said Pig.

"Get wet in my vat, Pig," said Fox.

"Not me!"
Pig ran.

Fox met Ox.
Fox wanted hot ox soup.

"What can I get?" said Ox.

"Get wet in my vat, Ox," said Fox.

"Not me!
I can not fit in a vat."

"Fox, you get in," said Ox.
"We can fix hot, hot fox soup!"

"Not hot fox soup!" said Fox.
"Let me fix hot, hot noodle soup."

"Is it hot yet, Fox?"

"Yes, it is hot, hot, hot," said Fox.
"Dig in!"

Think About the Story

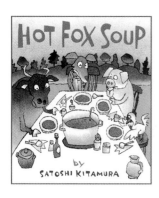

HOT FOX SOUP
by
SATOSHI KITAMURA

1 Why wouldn't the animals get in Fox's vat?

2 How did Ox surprise Fox?

3 Would you eat soup with Fox? Why?

Write a Sign

Make a sign with the words
Hot_____ Soup. Add your own
word to complete the sign.

Polly, Put

the Kettle On

Polly, put the kettle on,
Polly, put the kettle on,
Polly, put the kettle on,
We'll all have tea.

English Traditional Song

213

A Hut for Zig Bug

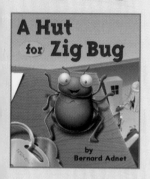

A Hut for Zig Bug
by Bernard Adnet

Teacher Read Aloud

California Standards

Standards I Can Achieve

Reading

- Blend sounds to read words (R1.10)
- Read sight words (R1.11)
- Story structure (R3.1)

214

Words to Know

does	fun
he	hut
live	jug
where	quit
Bug	rug
but	up
cup	Zig

Where does Zig Bug live?

Does he live in a hut?

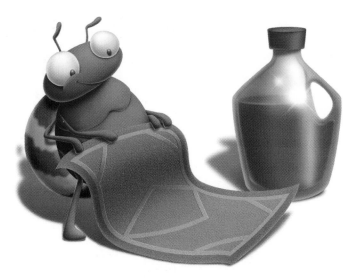

Zig Bug can get a jug.
Zig Bug can get a rug.

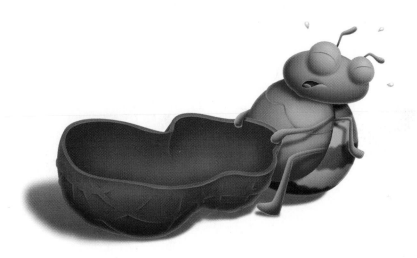

Do not quit!
Can Zig Bug fix up a fun hut?

Meet the Author and Illustrator
Bernard Adnet

A Hut for Zig Bug

by
Bernard Adnet

Does Zig Bug have a hut?
He does not have a hut yet.

Where can Zig Bug live?
Can he live in here?

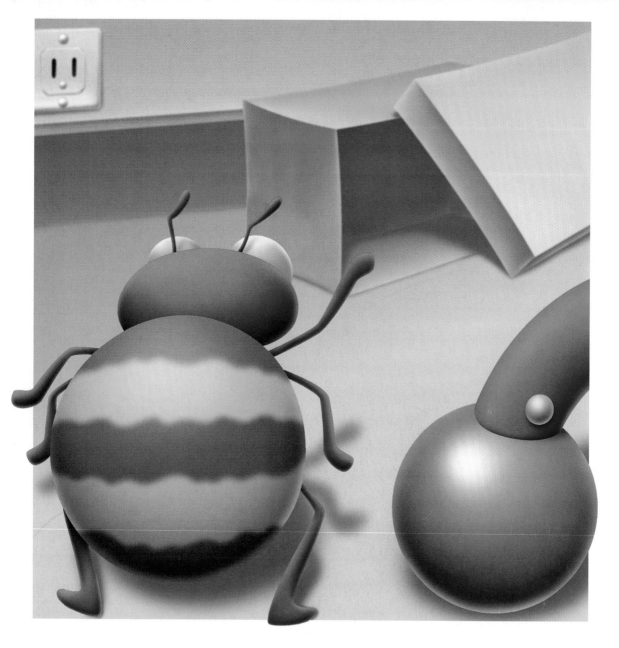

Can Zig Bug fix a box for a hut?
Yes, he can fix up a fun hut.

Can Zig Bug get a cot in the hut?

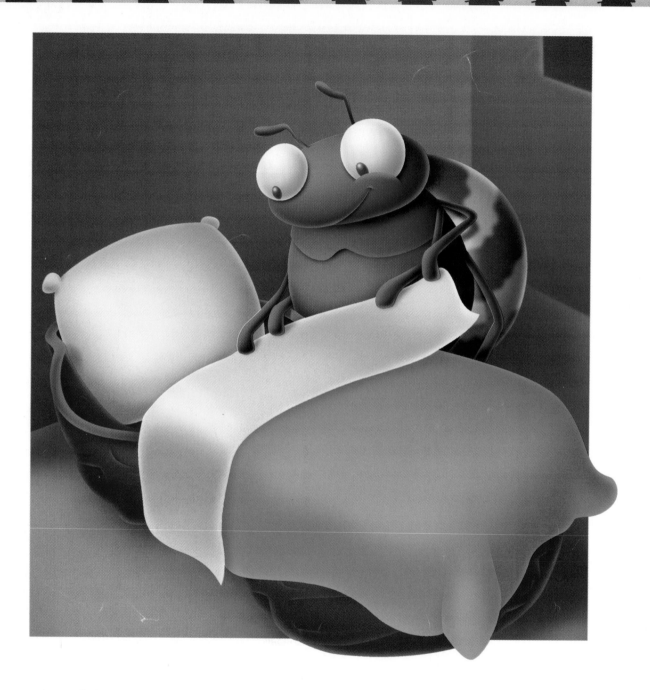

Yes, a cot can fit in the hut.

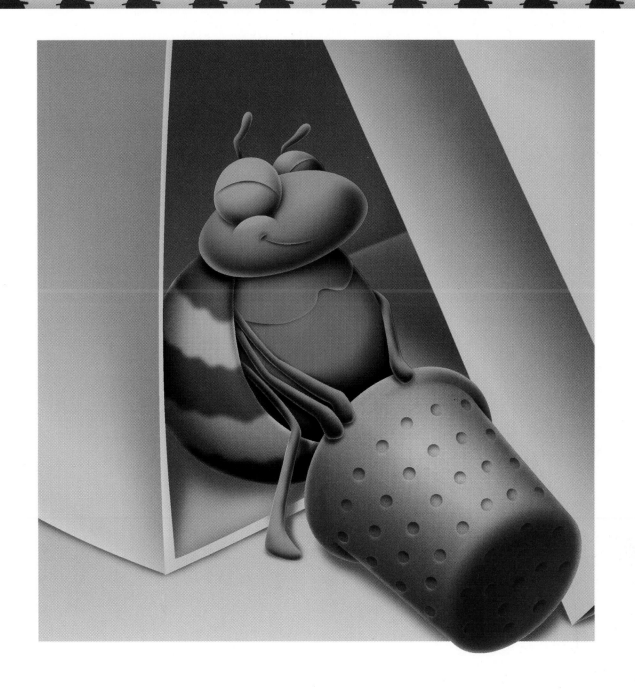

Can Zig Bug get a jug in the hut?

Yes, a jug can fit in the hut.
A cot and a jug can fit.

Can Zig Bug get a rug in the hut?

Yes, a rug can fit in the hut.
A cot, a jug, and a rug can fit.

Can Zig Bug get a cup in the hut?

Yes, a cup can fit in the hut.
A cot, a jug, a rug, and
a cup can fit.

Can Zig Bug fit in the hut?

Do not quit, Zig Bug!
You can fit!

Zig Bug does fit!
A cot, a jug, a rug, a cup,
and Zig Bug fit in the hut!

Think About the Story

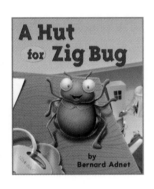

1 Was Zig Bug smart? Why?

2 What else could Zig Bug put in his hut?

3 Will Zig Bug be happy in his hut? Why?

Write a List

List the things Zig Bug put in his hut. Add some more things he could put in there.

The Rope Tug

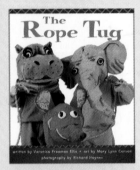

The **Rope Tug**

written by Veronica Freeman Ellis • art by Mary Lynn Carson
photography by Richard Haynes

Teacher Read Aloud

California Standards

Standards I Can Achieve

Reading

- Blend sounds to read words (R1.10)
- Read sight words (R1.11)
- Story structure (R3.1)

Words to Know

are	but	quit
away	hut	zag
does	jig	zig
pull	run	
they	tug	

Cat is in a big hut.
Rat does not run away.
Can Rat pull Cat?

Rat said, "You are big,
but I can tug!"
They tug, tug, tug.

"I quit," said Cat.
Rat does a jig.
Zig zag, zig zag!

Meet the Author
Veronica
Freeman Ellis

Meet the Artist
Mary Lynn
Carson

Meet the
Photographer
Richard Haynes

The Rope Tug

written by Veronica Freeman Ellis • art by Mary Lynn Carson
photography by Richard Haynes

Narrator

Elephant

Hippo

Rat

238

Elephant can get in the hut.
Hippo can get in the hut.

239

Rat can not get in.
Rat can not fit.

Let me in! Let me in!

You can not fit, Rat.
Run away, Rat!
Run, run, run!

 I can pull you outside.
I am not big, but I can tug.

242

 You can not tug me, Rat.

You can not tug me, Rat.

 Can you tug and pull me?
I am not big, but I can tug.

 We are big!
We can pull you!
Get a big rope, Rat!

 Rat can get a big, big rope.

 Rat can zig zag, zig zag.

 Tug, tug, tug!

 You can not win, Rat!
Tug, tug, tug!

They are big!
They tug and tug and tug,
but they can not pull Rat.

 I quit!

I quit!

 Rat does a jig.

I win! I win!
I'm not big, but I can tug!

251

Think About the Story

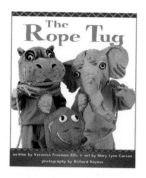

1 Why wouldn't Elephant and Hippo let Rat in the hut?

2 How did Rat surprise Elephant and Hippo?

3 How else could Rat have gotten Elephant and Hippo out of the hut?

Write a Description

Draw your favorite part of the play.
Write some words to tell about it.

Way Down South

Way down South where
   bananas grow,
A grasshopper stepped on
   an elephant's toe.
The elephant said, with tears
   in his eyes,
"Pick on somebody your
   own size."

Anonymous

254

Word Lists

The Cat Sat

Target Skills:

consonants *m, s, c, t*
Cat, Sam, sat

short *a*
Cat, Sam, sat

New
go, on, the

The Mat

Target Skills:

consonants *m, s, c, t*
Cam, Cat, mat, sat

short *a*
Cam, Cat, mat, sat

New
go, on, the

Nan and Fan

Target Skills:

consonants *n, f, p*
can, Fan, fat, Nan, pat, tap

short *a*
can, Fan, fat, Nan, pat, tap

Words Using Previously Taught Skills:
cat

SKILLS APPLIED IN WORDS IN STORY: consonants *c, t;* short *a*

New
and, not, jump

Previously Taught
go, the

257

We Can!

Target Skills:

consonants *n, f, p*

can, fan, Nat, Pam, Pat

short *a*

can, fan, Nat, Pam, Pat

SKILLS APPLIED IN WORDS IN STORY: consonants *m, c, t;* short *a*

HIGH–FREQUENCY WORDS

New

and, here, too, we

Previously Taught

go

STORY WORDS

draw, read, write

The Big Hit

DECODABLE WORDS

Target Skills:

consonants *b, r, h, g*

bam, bat, big, hit, ran, tag

short *i*

big, hit, Tim, Tip

Words Using Previously Taught Skills:

Cam, can, Nat, Pat, Sam

SKILLS APPLIED IN WORDS IN STORY: consonants *m, s, c, t;* short *a;* consonants *n, p*

HIGH–FREQUENCY WORDS

New

a, find, have, one, who

Previously Taught

go, not, the, we

258

Big Pig

Target Skills:

consonants *b, r, h, g*
Big, fig, hat, Pig, ran

short *i*
Big, fig, fit, Pig, sit, Tim

Words Using Previously Taught Skills:
can, fat, Nan, sat

SKILLS APPLIED IN WORDS IN STORY: consonants *m, s, c, t;* short *a;* consonants *n, f, p*

New
a, find, have, one, to, who

Previously Taught
and, go, on, the, too

farm, feed, carrot

Challenge Word
Chapter

The Box

Target Skills:

consonants *d, w, l, x*
box, Don, Dot, fox, lot, wig

short *o*
box, Don, Dot, fox, got, lot, top

Words Using Previously Taught Skills:
big, can, fit, hat, pig, tan

SKILLS APPLIED IN WORDS IN STORY: consonants *c, t;* short *a;* consonants *n, f, p;* consonants *b, h, g;* short *i*

New
in, once, what

Previously Taught
a, and, find, on, one, the

Wigs in a Box

Target Skills:

consonants *d, w, l, x*

box, Dog, Don, Dot, Fox, lot, Ox, wig, win

short *o*

box, Dog, Don, Dot, Fox, got, lot, Ox

Words Using Previously Taught Skills:

big, can, Cat, Fat, fit, hit, it, Pat, Pig, sat, Tan

SKILLS APPLIED IN WORDS IN STORY: consonants *s, c, t;* short *a;* consonants *n, f, p;* consonants *b, h, g;* short *i*

New

five, four, in, three, two, upon, what

Previously Taught

a, find, one, the

ball, shelf, thanks, wigs

What Can a Vet Do?

Target Skills:

consonants *k, v, y*

kit, van, vet, yes

short *e*

Ben, get, Ned, pen, pet, vet, wet, yes

Words Using Previously Taught Skills:

Big, bit, can, cat, fix, lot, Mom, pat, sit, tan

SKILLS APPLIED IN WORDS IN STORY: consonants *m, s, c, t;* short *a;* consonants *n, f, p;* consonants *b, g;* short *i;* consonants *d, w, l, x;* short *o*

New

do, for, is, my

Previously Taught

a, here, in, jump, not, the, to, what

Challenge Word

Chapter

260

Hot Fox Soup

Target Skills:

consonants _k, v, y_
kit, vat, yes, yet

short _e_
get, hen, let, met, wet, yes, yet

Words Using Previously Taught Skills:
big, box, can, dig, fit, fix, fox, got, hot, it, lit, ox, pig, ran

SKILLS APPLIED IN WORDS IN STORY: consonants _m, s, c, t;_ short _a;_ consonants _n, f, p;_ consonants _b, r, h, g;_ short _i;_ consonants _d, w, l, x;_ short _o_

HIGH-FREQUENCY WORDS

New
I, is, me, my, said, you

Previously Taught
a, in, not, we, what

STORY WORDS
fire, noodle, soup, wanted

A Hut for Zig Bug

DECODABLE WORDS

Target Skills:

consonants _q, j, z_
jug, quit, Zig

short _u_
Bug, cup, fun, hut, jug, rug, up

Words Using Previously Taught Skills:
box, can, cot, fit, fix, get, yes, yet

SKILLS APPLIED IN WORDS IN STORY: consonants _s, c, t;_ short _a;_ consonants _n, f, p;_ consonants _b, r, h, g;_ short _i;_ consonant _x;_ short _o;_ consonant _y;_ short _e_

HIGH-FREQUENCY WORDS

New
does, he, live, where

Previously Taught
a, and, do, for, have, here, in, not, the, you

The Rope Tug

Target Skills:

consonants *q, j, z*
jig, quit, zag, zig

short *u*
but, hut, run, tug

Words Using Previously Taught Skills:
am, big, can, get, fit, let, Rat, win

SKILLS APPLIED IN WORDS IN STORY: consonants *m, c, t;* short *a;* consonants *n, f;* consonants *b, r, h, g;* short *i;* consonants *w, l;* short *e*

New
are, away, does, pull, they

Previously Taught
a, and, I, in, me, not, the, we, you

Elephant, Hippo, I'm, Narrator, outside, rope

HIGH-FREQUENCY WORDS TAUGHT TO DATE

a	here	said
and	I	the
are	in	they
away	is	three
do	jump	to
does	live	too
find	me	two
five	my	upon
for	not	we
four	on	what
go	once	where
have	one	who
he	pull	you

Decoding skills taught to date: consonants *m, s, c, t;* short *a;* consonants *n, f, p;* consonants *b, r, h, g;* short *i;* consonants *d, w, l, x;* short *o;* consonants *k, v, y;* short *e;* consonants *q, j, z;* short *u*

Acknowledgments

For each of the selections listed below, grateful acknowledgment is made for permission to excerpt and/or reprint original or copyrighted material, as follows:

Poetry

"At Night" from *Out in the Dark and Daylight,* by Aileen Fisher. Copyright © 1980 by Aileen Fisher. Used by permission of Marian Reiner for the author.

"Cats" by Jacquiline Kirk. Copyright © by Jacquiline Kirk. Reprinted by permission of the author.

"Here Is the Beehive" from *Hand Rhymes,* collected and illustrated by Marc Brown. Copyright © 1985 by Marc Brown. Published by Dutton Children's Books, a division of Penguin Putnam Inc.

"Riddle" from *The Llama Who Had No Pajama: 100 Favorite Poems,* by Mary Ann Hoberman. Copyright © 1973 by Mary Ann Hoberman. Reprinted by permission of Harcourt Inc.

"There was a small pig who wept tears . . ." from *The Book of Pigericks: Pig Limericks,* by Arnold Lobel. Copyright © 1983 by Arnold Lobel. Reprinted by permission of HarperCollins Publishers.

"Together" from *Embrace: Selected Love Poems,* by Paul Engle. Copyright © 1969 by Paul Engle. Reprinted by permission of Random House, Inc.

Credits

Photography

CA4 (frog) JH Pete Carmichael/ImageBank. **CA5** (hat, school bus) © 2001 PhotoDisc. (butterfly) Artville. (shuttle) Comstock KLIPS. (caterpillar) © Michael & Patricia Fogden/CORBIS. **3** (t) image Copyright © 2000 PhotoDisc, Inc. **7** (t) image Copyright © 2000 PhotoDisc, Inc. **12** (icon) image Copyright © 2000 PhotoDisc, Inc. **12–13** Jo Browne/Mick Samee/Tony Stone Images. **16** Courtesy Lynn Munsinger. **27** (cat) Artville. **30** Courtesy NB Westcott. **44** Artville. **46–7** Artville. **50** Courtesy Lisa Campbell Ernst. **64** (l) American Images Inc./FPG International. (r) Jeri Gleiter/FPG International. **68** (t) Lawrence Migdale. (b) Mark Gardner. **82** images Copyright © 2000 PhotoDisc, Inc. **84–5** Telegraph Colour Library/FPG International. **88** Andrew Yates/Mercury Pictures. **89** Dennis Gray/Mercury Pictures. **104** images Copyright © 2000 PhotoDisc, Inc. **108** Sharron McElmeel. **124** images Copyright © 2000 PhotoDisc, Inc. **125** (r) image Copyright © 2000 PhotoDisc, Inc. **128** (icon) image Copyright © 2000 PhotoDisc, Inc. **128–9** Mauritius/Nawrocki Stock Photo Inc. **132** (t) Jon Crispin/Mercury Pictures. (b) Courtesy Cynthia Jabar. **150** Courtesy Valeria Petrone. **170** (t) Kindra Clineff. (b) Courtesy Anne Kennedy. **186** image Copyright © 2000 PhotoDisc, Inc. **190** Courtesy Farrar, Straus and Giroux. **210** image Copyright © 2000 PhotoDisc, Inc. **216** Courtesy Bernard Adnet. **236** (t) Jesse Nemerofksy/Mercury Pictures.

Assignment Photography

CA1 (t) Joel Benjamin. (b) Tony Scarpetta. **CA2** (t) Allan Landau. **CA3** Tony Scarpetta. **CA4** (t) Allan Landau. (b) Tony Scarpetta. **CA5** Joel Benjamin. **66–67, 69–81** Joel Benjamin. **26–7, 45, 65, 83, 105, 125** (l), **146–7, 164–5, 166–7, 187, 211, 232–3, 253** David Bradley Photographer. **234–5, 236** (m&b), **237–252** Richard Haynes.

Illustration

14–25 Lynn Munsinger. **28–43** Nadine Wescott. **48–63** Lisa Campbell Ernst. **70–81**(t) Rob Dunlavey. **86–103** John Ceballos. **106–123** David McPhail. **126–127** Stef De Reuver. **130–145** Cynthia Jabar. **148–163** Valerie Petrone. **166–167** Tammy Smith. **168–185** Anne Kennedy. **188–209** Satoshi Kitamura. **212–213** Matt Novak. **214–231** Bernard Adnet. **234–251** Mary Lynn Carson. **254–255** Keiko Motoyama.